A LIBERATED WOMAN
FROM THE GHETTO

A LIBERATED WOMAN FROM THE GHETTO

✦

One Woman Production

Written and Performed by
ELEANOR CURRY

iUniverse, Inc.
New York Lincoln Shanghai

A LIBERATED WOMAN FROM THE GHETTO
One Woman Production

iUniverse books may be ordered through booksellers or by contacting:

iUniverse
2021 Pine Lake Road, Suite 100
Lincoln, NE 68512
www.iuniverse.com
1-800-Authors (1-800-288-4677)

Because of the dynamic nature of the Internet, any Web addresses or links contained in this book may have changed since publication and may no longer be valid.

The views expressed in this work are solely those of the author and do not necessarily reflect the views of the publisher, and the publisher hereby disclaims any responsibility for them.

Eleanor Curry presented A Liberated Woman from the Ghetto on October 3, 1975, at the Main Theatre at Canada College in Redwood City, California.

A Revised and Expanded Version from the Original

ISBN: 978-0-595-46804-1 (pbk)
ISBN: 978-0-595-91094-6 (ebk)

Printed in the United States of America

Dedicated to you

Ready to laugh relax and enjoy a little more good living.

Contents

SCENE ONE IDENTITIES 1

SCENE TWO DISCOVERY. 11

SCENE THREE MATURITY. 23

PLACES WE HAVE LIVED 27

PEOPLE KEPT ASKING ME QUESTIONS 29

ABOUT THE AUTHOR 37

Scenery and lighting by Bob Miller and Doreen Adamson. Costumes designs and choreography by Eleanor Curry.

The action was based on some reflective life experiences that spans the ages. It was performed with two ten-minute musical interludes between the three scenes.

Musical Advisor, Bob Miller

The Characters in Order of Appearance

Eleanor	Self Portrait
Martha Mix-up	Radio Announcer
Earl Hard Hat	the Philosopher
Eleanor	the Traveler

SCENE ONE
IDENTITIES

Curry (G)

Prelude: Sophisticated Lady ... Music by Duke Ellington

The curtain rises. Spotlight—Right Stage
Character dressed in several layers of clothes that are to be removed as
Identity goes full circle.

Eleanor (as self) "Good evening, Human persons, descendents and oth-
ers. My name is Eleanor Curry. I am from the 'Show Me State'. I have
seen enough of Missouri. So now I will let the state show me. Any con-
nection that you see between persons living and working near me will
be for real and furthermore it will be true.

"Did you know that there are three kinds of truths that can expose you?
Gospel, drunk or naked. (Pause) I never lie. (Pause) That is the gospel
truth. I always tell the truth, except when I'm drunk. Either way, it's
the bare facts. Speaking about gospel, I want to tell you about a dream I
had. It's called 'The Creation'. This took place only between three people; GOD, Lucifer and Madame Chairperson."

Monologue: The Creation

Madam Chairperson: (Sitting at a desk, preparing for a public meeting. She speaks to no one in particular). Now that I have cunning, devious Lucifer under control, I shall be out front, in the center and in charge. He's the most manipulative person I've yet. Well, at least he's down there where he can't do us too much harm. Maybe he'll have sense enough to just push a few buttons to keep that fireplace burning. (The telephone rings).

Madam Chairperson: Hello, this is the HEAP organization, Madam speaking, may I help you? Oh! Lucifer. What do you want? What does HEAP mean? You know what HEAP stands for—Heavenly Environmental Agency to Protect.

Protect us against what? That's obvious—Against whatever is coming. (Pause.) Yes we are having a meeting tonight. Yes it is too late to get on the agenda. It takes at least 24 hours, and you know that. You say you have some mail that cannot wait? Oh, A MALE? (Interested now) What's his name? He claims he's who? GOD? Look Lucifer, HEAP has enough problems without you making up … O.K. O.K. I'm listening. You have a report from TV that says the world did not start with an apple on the tree? It was a pear on the ground? (Bewildered voice) The creatures started to use a banana, but the banana split? Lucifer you're way off the subject again! What does GOD wants from us? GOD said he has created heaven and earth and He wants to file a statement with HEAP so HIS plans can be carried forth. Sounds like he will need two applications; one for Heaven and one for Earth.

What do you mean not Earth? Do you think GOD means Heaven and Hell? Heaven is already full of Spirits! You mean earth is full of spirits. Where does Hell fit in? Lucifer, why don't you just describe Hell. You say 'It's void, empty right now and very dark, it's like a dungeon? Really? O.K. I will give GOD a temporary permit for Heaven, and nothing for that Hell territory. What do you mean, this is a sticky situation? I could turn down the whole thing! After all, I am in charge! So you think GOD is getting disturbed? Well, I've been disturbed all my life. GOD hates red tape? Lucifer, stop trying to tempt me. You have not been talking to GOD. Here's my last position on your scheming confusing plan. Heaven yes. Hell no.

A loud deep voice: Madam Chairperson.
(Madam C. gets excited, stutters, stammers, looks up, moves in a spin, looks around, and then stands still).
Madam C. speaks with surprise: "Oh! my goodness! (Then a bright humble greeting) How are you doing GOD? I knew you would come to the ghetto one of these days. Lucifer called trying to tempt me. I told him Hell No!! What are your plans, Father? I'm ready!

Deep Voice: "I want you to know Hell is already in place. I must conquer the darkness."

Madam C. "Makes sense to me. I'm listening; I'm making notes to get every word you say."
Deep Voice: When I raised my hand light came upon the earth. This light has been made by my power. This light came from a large ball of fire."

Madam C.: "Did that cause a lot of smoke and smog? One more thing! How did you cover the earth?"

DeepVoice: "With firmament. Amidst the waters, and with the waters and the waterfalls I have creatures crawling over the earth and fouls in the air and all manner of things."

Madam C.: Wait a minute. You sound like you do need some help. (Picks up the phone). Get a permit from the Neutral Angelic Association on Community Planning. (Pause) Yes, that permit is under the NAACP listing. You'd better get a Water Permit, too. We need something about the light, hold on!

(Looking up) Sir, what was that about the light? Will there be any darkness? I think a little darkness won't hurt. There's only so much you can do in the light.

Deep Voice: "I raised my hand, called the light day and the darkness night."

Madam C.: "Any other future developments?"

Deep Voice: "Yes. On the 6th day, I shall make me a man."

Madam C.: "What about us?

Deep Voice: "I shall create woman for the good of man."

Madam C.: "What? Are you kidding me?"

Deep Voice: "You shall be good for man, yourself and other living things!"

Madam C.: "Forget it! I mean, really GOD. I love you. I was expecting something better from you. I know you can do everything. Now I'm hearing the same old story. Sounds to me like only a man can be liberated and free. (Total silence for 5 seconds) She walks back to her desk, picks up some papers, looks up)
I'm sorry God for asking those questions. You took six days to build creation. Who am I to doubt the rest of your plans? When do you need these permits?

Deep Voice: I have done the biggest part in six days. I want it today!"

Madam C.: "What? Your timing is way off! . It will take me a month to place you on the next agenda.

First, you are going to have a Son before then, and he's going to need some diapers.

Second, just to process your application will take centuries. Look at all this. The people claimed they found some new properties in a place called the United States and the Indians already owned the land!

Third, do you realize all the folks I have to get together for the public hearings on your plans? The Ku Klux Klan, the Civil Rights leaders, the Orientals and the Mexicans. You know the Unions stay upset if their people don't do the work. Besides, I didn't even get to the Democrats and the Republicans yet.

Fourth, you won't be able to get a Permit before the year 2000.

(Roaring noise, thunders and lightning flashing)

Deep Voice: "Vengeance is mine."

Madam C.: (Rushes to the phone, dials 911 swiftly and shouts) "Push the buttons to lighten the earth. GOD is pouring sheets of rain for forty days and forty nights. What do you mean the button is stuck? Well, hurry up. Push the other button then and lower Heaven."

Curtain closes

Monologue # 2 IDENTITIES (Continued)

Many of us are always searching for identity, and wonder, 'Who am I?' I looked around and found a poem called "I Am Many Of Me". Here's my version of that poem.

SERIOUS: I am a slave woman. Just gave birth to Master's son today. Gotta pick cotton anyway. I been <u>had.</u> But that's all right, it won't be for long, 'cause when I'm alone I sing my song. (Sings) Steal away, steal away. Steal away to Jesus. Steal away, steal away home. I ain't got long to stay here.

PROUD: I am a servant. I help prepare food for me who do not like me. Yet they are crazy enough to let me fix their food. I am so <u>glad.</u> But I wouldn't do anything to them anyway, cause I know about judgement day. Let me tell you something else. (Sings) His eye is on the sparrow and I know he watches me.

GAILY: I am a lady of noble ancestry drivin' along in my red hog. Honey, I dig this <u>fad.</u> (Claps and sings.) I'm a St. Louis woman with her diamond rings, (Them ain't diamonds, those are stones.) I drive all over the town and I don't miss a thing.

SWINGING: I am a student going to college to study hi-er-o-gly-phics, so we can overcome. I must be a <u>grad.</u> (Sings.) "School days, school days, good old-fashioned rule days. Reading' and writing' and 'arithmetic', taught to the tune of a hickory stick. You were my beau and I was your gal, (Turns to the audience: I bet you never thought I'd graduate from CAL) and this is why I loved you so when we were a couple of kids."

ANGRY: I am a mother, trying to explain to Susie why she was not invited to Ann's party. They just did not want any black folks there. I am so <u>mad.</u> Don't worry Susie, because you can have your own dreams. Just remember honey, (Sings) "Some where over the rainbow, skies are blue and the dreams that you dare to dream, really do come true."

BOASTFUL: I am YES, the black's man natural love. Do you know what? He thinks I have castrated him. Too bad he won't face the facts. I get so <u>sad.</u> He works hard all day. He gets frustrated about that small paycheck. He comes home and says to me, "Caledonia, Caledonia, what makes your big head so hard?" I say right back, (sings) Straighten up and fly right. Straighten up and fly right. Straighten up and fly right. Cool down Poppa don't you blow your top.

STOMPS HER FOOT: Yes, I am many of me. All my yesterdays, today and all my Tomorrows, wrapped up in the sight you see because (sings). I can see clearly now, the rain is gone. I can see all obstacles in my way. Gone are the dark clouds that had me blind. It's gonna be bright, bright, bright sun shiny days. Let me tell you honey. I AM SUPER BAD.

Well, that was a little like me. But I truly want to be a radio announcer. (Transition: Changes to a jacket and a wig. Picks up a microphone and becomes Martha Mix-up)

RADIO STATION TIT for TAT. This is Martha Mix-up, Ghetto City, B.C.A. That's Black Country of America. Our information comes from the most reliable sources. Reliable sources are everybody who tells us the truth, as long as we don't use their name. Now to the news. The citizens of the ghetto, that's we; are returning all Robert Rules of Order books back to the Suburbs; that's them. Those books didn't work for us either. Did you know Mother Goose was really a political pigeon who loved pets? She always thought old Mother Hubbard should have food stamps for her dog, too. Mother Goose came to the ghetto one day said to the little children,

> "What are little girls made of? Blood, bones and skin, all colors are in the ghetto. But be careful when you go out of the ghetto."

Here's a news flash from Capitol Hill. The President called the Congressional Black Caucus together. He wanted a definition for unemployment. They made a most profound statement. "Unemployment is not working."

The fact for the day is, in case you didn't know it, that the universal language is not English. It is profanity and everybody gives a damage.

Question of the day: A man went to a therapist and said, "My wife and I are slowly drifting apart. Can you suggest something that will speed it up?"
"You must need a motor on your boat. Sounds like you are at low tide."

Advice for the day is on freeway driving: There's only one way to drive on the freeway; FAST. Here's another tip. Always go to your destination early, and enjoy the scenery once you get lost. Just because you have been there once before, doesn't prove a thing. I'd been to Mills College in Oakland no less than 5 times. Guess what happen six months later? They moved the freeway.

Here are some hot tips to any woman going into management. All major decisions are made in four rooms. God's room, the backroom, the barroom and the conference room.

If your computer gets stuck or runs out or paper, call the key operator, operator, operator.

Regardless of what you decide to wear, the weather will change, whether you like it or not. This is Martha Mix-up, Ghetto City, B.C.A.

SCENE TWO
DISCOVERY

(Roll of the Drums) Stand still. Center Stage, Count 3 seconds. Hands on waist. Speak precise and clear. Next Male Character moves to Center stage.

"Hi, I'm Earl Hard Hat. I'm going to let you in on a little secret. There are a lot of crazy people running around loose in this country today. And I married to one of them. Tonight you're going to hear the truth about her. Some things you won't believe. For one thing, she thinks she's free. She told me she had enrolled in College! I'm shocked. Man, she is 48 years old. She keeps telling people she is 29 years old. To top that off when she enrolled in College she came home excited as could be. She said, "Guess what?" She was lit up like our Christmas tree, but it was only September. "I am a full-fledged student." She was so happy I didn't have the heart to discourage her.

"Are you cooking dinner tonight?" I asked calmly as possible. "OH, she turned to me very surprised, "Students don't have time to cook. We have to study." She hugged me, gave me a peck on my cheek and left the room.

I was stunned. We still have three teenage sons at home, who need to eat her home-cooked meals. I'm still working every day. I have to have my dinner ready in the evening promptly at 5:00 PM. like she's been

11

doing for the past 25 years. To tell the truth I think she is already smart enough. Of course, I'm keeping that to myself. I want her to stay humble and not get a swelled head. You know what I mean?

Before I tell about Eleanor's strange behavior, I want to tell you about my country.

Man, this country is something else. Am I right? This country has everything anybody ever wanted? Do you agree with me? Let me explain what I mean. We have laws, hope and religion. We can move and travel anywhere we want to. We have all kind of stuff. And most of these people still ain't happy. Something must be wrong with them. Let me tell you something. There are probably a few things wrong with this country. I'd be the first to admit it, but there's a whole lot right with it. Don't you agree? Are you hearing me? (Audience hollers back "YES!" Well make me know it. Let me tell you about this country and how I feel. All you have to do is believe. Your belief can be as tiny as a little mustard seed. It says so right in the good book. A little mustard seed. It gives good directions too.

What's clearer than this? Ask and it shall be given. Too many people messed that one up. They thought it said tell what you want and take it. Next came seek and you shall find. Did you hear me? Seek and you shall find. They ruined that one. They thought it said search for other people's stuff and seize it. Listen to this. Knock and it will be opened. Do you know what too many people are doing with that? They thought it said knock everything over until it's beyond repair.

I'll tell you something else I believe. I believe in the Constitution. That's right. Wait, I forgot about the Ten Commandments. These are ten good rules anybody can follow. Either you are going to follow them, or you are not. Many people act like they never even heard them. Some people think they are so smart, they made an 11th Commandment. "And don't get caught." That was broken too. Look at Watergate. All of them got caught.

I believe in voting, the Constitution and the Bill of Rights. Tell me one thing. What could be more beautiful than these words? "We hold these truths to be self-evident, that all men are created equal and endowed by their creator." You know who that is don't you? (Pause) That's GOD … O.K. where was I? With certain inalienable rights that among these are life, liberty and the pursuit of happiness." I have to admit one thing. The authors really blew that part. Do you think they understood what they meant to say? It said 'the pursuit of happiness.' Did you get that line? Happiness was never, never promised, just its pursuit.

Anybody out here tonight have any kids? Some of you folks do have kids. Man. Ah—sweet miserables of life. We have eight kids. (Pause) They are all on the Bell-Shaped Curve. Don't get me wrong. Some of our kids are smart. But they can act so dumb just like our other relatives. No, I didn't say my wife. You know what gets to me the most? Asking me dumb questions? Man, did you ever come home from work tired and hungry? You think how great it is to finally be home. You put your key in the lock, turn the knob, and open the door. The house is in shambles. The record player is going full blast. There's not any dinner smelling. You open the refrigerator, and somebody drank the last can of beer. Hopeless you stand in the middle of the kitchen and you shout, "Where is everybody?" Suddenly the kids and the wife appear. "What's the matter Daddy? "Why are you talking so loud dear? Is something bothering you?" My wife looked concerned. "Who? Me?" I responded ready to roar. "What could be bothering me? I'm just hungry, tired and thirsty. That's all." My wife glanced at me relieved and said, "Oh, is that all? I thought you had an accident or something terrible had happened." Remember I told you my wife is a little crazy? Change that to very crazy!

This next story you will not believe. We had trouble with some of our kids learning how to read. I told them to go to school, listen to the teacher and you'll learn how to read. Your mother knows how to read. I know how to read. We are your natural born parents; it makes no sense that you don't know how to read. The message worked on all except one seven years old son. He was in the second grade. I came home from work, when I heard the news about him. He was ready to cry. After dinner, I figured I could get this over quick. So I sat him on my lap, got a big sheet of paper and a pencil. I said ABCDEFG. When we reached the letter 'I', he asked me. "Does that mean you Daddy?" "No, son it means 'I'. "That's what I said Daddy. 'I' means you." When we reached the letter 'U'. I'd say 'U'. He'd say "Me, daddy?" looking puzzled. I'd say 'No, not you, just 'U'. "Just me, Daddy?"

"Eleanor", I called perplexed, and slightly annoyed "You know I have to work. I have to get a little relaxation before I go to work tomorrow. I know you have a lot to do, but you have enough kids who know how to read. So let one of them teach him how to read. It is simple as that."

The first daughter said, "Come on there's nothing to it. You can read right after me." One week later, he still was not reading. The second teenage daughter rather annoyed, said to him, "Hurry up boy. I don't have all day. Are you just pretending to be stupid?" He started to cry. The third teenage daughter walked in, gave him a hug and said, "Reading is fun. All you have to do is say what I say." They seemed to have less friction. After two weeks she wondered if he really belonged in this family. He was very confused about nouns; verbs and anything connected to spelling.

He came home from school after trying for a whole month and my husband said ..." (Hot dog! I am my husband). I said, "Eleanor, let that boy alone. He'll read in his own time, in his own way."

Another week passed by. This time he was excited. "Hey Mommy. Guess what? I know how to read now." Eleanor bent down to hug him, asking him, "What did you do?"
"I bought me a book in Spanish."

Have any of you heard about psychology? Do you know what psychology is? Psychology is a way to psyche people out of misery. I've got one sixteen-year-old son who reads all day long. He has never had any kind of job in his life. The wife thinks he's brilliant. I connect that word with people who earn a salary, even if they are underage. This boy reads at school, at home, on the bus, anywhere he can stand still. Keep in mind I'm working all day, from 7:30 AM to 4:30 PM. I wondered what in the world could he be reading. I soon found out. He had this psychology book telling him how to get along with people. I parked my truck right in front of his mother. She came in before me. He tried the new stuff on her first.

"Hi, Mom. How are you doing today?" he asked cheerfully.
"Hello", Eleanor said waiting for the next comment.
"Did you have a nice day?"
"It went pretty good. What's up with these questions?"

"Oh, nothing. I'm glad you had a beautiful day. No I don't need anything." He said smiling.

Next, I enter the same door.
"Hello Dad. How are you doing today?" he asked beaming.
"What the devil you mean. How am I doing today? You must be kidding. How would you feel if you had been working all day out in the cold and the drizzling rain? Trying to keep food in your stomach and a roof over your head? What do you mean how do I feel?"
"Sorry, Dad." He glanced at his mother for support. You know what she did? She laughed and started singing "Let it be ..." I realized right then. Insanity is inherited. You get it from your kids.

Have you heard about all these children who keep running away from home? We can't get any of our kids to leave. In fact they even have the nerve to bring their friends over to eat and spend the night. I said to the wife. "Please tell your kids this is not Grand Central Station. When I filed my last Income tax statement I thought we were taking care of somebody else' s family. I was right.

Let me tell you something else. I've got grandchildren too. One day, my 8 year old grandson came up to me. They call me Poppa Curry.

"Papa Curry, Papa Curry." He said eagerly.

"What do you want boy?" I replied based on how they sound. If they are about to cry, I send them to their grandmother.

"Papa Curry. Do you know you got three flags on your hard hat?"

"Yea, man, I put them up there."

"What do they stand for?"

"They stand for my political views!"

"Do you need all three of them?"

"Of course," I said, getting a little annoyed.

"Well could you tell me what they mean?"

"It means whether the issues are on the right, or on the left or dead center, my politics might be all three. You have to stay informed."

His grandmother shows up only to hear the end of the talk. She said to me. "Stop confusing the boy, honey."

Oh, and now to my wife. Remember when folks were running around here not knowing who they were? I thought everybody knew who I was. I'm a carpenter and Foreman at my job. They hired a new white fellow. He had been working as a teacher in education, I guess. He must have needed some extra money. So he decided to become a carpenter. He was surprised to see a black foreman.

"What are you calling yourself these days?" He asked me. He seemed sincere.

"I call myself Earl Hard Hat," I replied extending my right hand to greet him.

"I mean Negro, colored people or black?" He was dead serious.

I'm nonplussed, thinking to myself 'What kind of nut is this?' I say out loud,

"Society is always starting something it can't finish, you know what I mean?

Forget what to call me. It's time to work. This is job you have to do today."

I thought about those questions as I finished working. I could hardly wait to get home. I hope my teenage kids are not as confused as that fellow was. I've got to straighten my kids out in case these stupid remarks are floating around the high school. We are going to have a serious talk right after dinner.

"Eleanor bring all these kids in the dining room again. I want to get something straight right now." They entered unexcited and dutiful. I know. I know. They hate some of my little friendly talks. But this is another important one. Once the wife has them quiet and ready we begin the conversation.

"There's a lot of questions flying around from people who don't know who we are. They probably don't know who they are either. Just so you'll know who you are, I'll tell you right now!"

"Honey, we can hear you, "the wife said interrupting as usual.

"Let me finish my statement." I said determined and a little louder. "Before I was so rudely interrupted." I'm lowering my voice a little. "I want my kids to know who all of you are. We are the architects of God's being, created in his own image. You are, they are, your mother is and I am. Now who are we to question God's masterful work? You got that clear? Don't let people be confusing you with all that talk, wondering if you are calling yourself Negroes, black, or colored people."

You know most kids don't want to hear nothing you tell them for their good. They have this expression on their faces implying something is wrong with you.

"Hey, Dad," my oldest son was getting ready to answer back. "I hate to disagree with you ..." "Well, don't!" I said quickly.

You know what the wife said, right in front of me to my kids?

"Your father means in this house, according to your birth certificates, you shall be known as the Hard Hat family. We used to be called coloreds. But outside, you can go anywhere in this country, and pass for a black person."

I'm not sure if I won or lost that conversation. Amazing how she changes things.

It is also amazing how she acts. She never seems to know when to stop. I mean never. When I first met her, I told my best friend, "I'm going to marry that girl." We went out on a couple dates. The closer I got to her the better I liked her.

"Hey, baby, let's get married and have a house full of kids" I said. "I came from a family of three sisters and six brothers."

"Really?" she asked excited, yet not completely convinced, but said, "O.K."

Five kids later, she was sitting on our front porch on a hot spring day in St. Louis, Missouri. It was 97 degrees. I was off from work that day. She gave me a spunky glance.

"You know what?" She asked and kept talking. "Remember when we met and you told me, 'let's get married and have a bunch of kids?'

"Yes." I said waiting for her to finish.

"If I had known you was serious, I wouldn't have married you."

"Listen, if I'd known you didn't have enough sense to know when to stop, I wouldn't have married you either."

Guess what she did after that little talk? She got on the Planned Parenthood Board. But it was too late. We had two more children after that. Sure is hard to break a good bad habit.

Eleanor is also full of excuses. I love my wife when she cooks. I tell you I feel very excited all over. She was cooking dinner, and the aroma from the food would catch any hungry person's nostrils. I came up behind her, and put my arms around her. I was feeling in the mood. You know what I mean?

"Hey, baby, you know what I just realized?" I kept talking. "You never asked me to make love to you."

"You never gave me a chance!" she turned and said surprised.

So I waited five minutes. She put me on hold until later. Later is worse than waiting for tomorrow.

You already must know my wife always has to have the last word. One week she had to go to four night meetings. It was the church, or the Parents Teachers Association or one of the kids' Counseling Sessions. Here I am just coming in the door from work

She met me at the door, kissed me too quick and was ready to go. I grabbed her arm.
"Another Russian meal tonight?" She stopped and asked

"Russian? I cooked spaghetti and French bread for dinner."

"No, you rushed the groceries from the store, to the stove, to the table and now at me." I said slowly hoping she would linger for a few minutes.

She threw her head back laughing heartily, grabbed her Reports; paused at the front door and said, "at least it beats a Polish Breakfast."

"What's that?" I asked a little bewildered.

"Cold Tongue!" She exclaimed, slamming the door.

By now you figured out I have to be married. I have a few tips that I picked up. Watch out for those promises, promises, and more promises. Man, promises cost a lot of money! This is her main thought on money. 'Money is not everything. It's not even enough.' My views, since I'm the only one working, are on target. Money does make a dif-

ference. If you have two jobs and you're rich, you have diversified inter-
ests. If you have two jobs and you're poor, you're moonlighting. My
wife thinks I'm both. Rich in spirit and poor in green bucks. She thinks
a budget is living beyond our yearnings.

Don't get me wrong. I love my wife; my kids and I certainly love my
country. Are you hearing me? Everything who loves this country over
here, (pointing to the right side) clap your hands. Everybody who loves
kids right here (pointing to the center) clap your hands. Everybody
with a wife to love, (pointing to the left) over here clap your hands.
What did I say? Are you clapping? Yes! Yes! Yes! (The telephone rings
and rings)

"Excuse me for a second. Hello? No my wife is not here. Would you
care to leave a rumor? You heard from her and she's going where? Is she
going to the bicentennial to tap-dance? I hope not.
Thank you very much. Yeah. Goodbye." As I told you way back, there's
a bunch of crazy people running loose and I know I'm married to one
of them."

(The lights fade away)

MUSICAL INTERLUDE
SCENE THREE
MATURITY

Finding the Hidden Me

The Queen looked into her mirror and said "Mirror, mirror on the wall, who's the fairest of them all?"
"You are my Queen," the little mirror answered back.

Just recently the President of our country took his mirror, patted his hair back and said,
"Mirror, Mirror on this wall, I am the President, I am. I am. I am. I will run this hall."

"Not anymore, dear President, "the mirror said back. "You are about to fall."

Now if this mirror can give these kinds of reactions, I need to see what it might say to me.

"Mirror, mirror on the wall, why do I look round like a ball?"

And the mirror said:

> "Mirrors, mirrors are reflections to be
> What you are, is what you see
> Maybe there's too much of thee.
>
> HMMM, looking at you, as you are
> Maybe your size has spread too far
> Large is not small
> But round like a ball
> So all in all …
> Woman, you have to lose some weight."

So I better get with a program, one more time. I had been on diets now and then, for 15 years. I hate counting calories and measuring ounces. This time I'm going for the easy one. The Water Diet. Do all of you know about that one? Anybody can drink 8 glasses of water a day. That's only one glass of water an hour, going in! I only have to be on my job a mere 8 hours a day. The first day starts with one glass of water an hour plus two coffee breaks. The second day on the diet I had twelve water breaks. I had water on my mind even when I was not drinking any water. The secretary said our Manager was taking orders for any new office equipment.

"Ask for a new toilet next to my office." The Manager overheard me talking.

"Eleanor there is only one toilet for the Executive Office. I have it near my office until I finish this blasted water diet." He stated ready to dash to the bathroom.

After that episode, I made some adjustments to my plans. I decided to drink 3 glasses of water from 8AM to 5 PM and the rest in the evening after dinner. I've always been a sound sleeper. Four years after I was married, my husband sent me to the Doctor to find out why I could go to sleep so fast. After hearing my schedule, the doctor told me I was blessed being able to sleep so natural without any sedatives.

I'm drinking more water after dinner. No big thing except, I'm waking up at 2 A.M. in the morning. I had to go to the John. I eased out of bed, so I wouldn't wake up my husband.

"Eleanor, are you alright?" He turned over, rubbing his eyes.

"Yes," I half whispered, "I'm just going to the John." He jumped straight up in the bed.

"What's John doing here this time of night?"

"No, honey, I'm going to the John, you know the bathroom!"

"Girl! Why don't you just say toilet?" He snatched the cover back over his head trying to shut out the stream of light from the bathroom.

Ten pounds and five days later, I had to give up this Water Diet. I had water on my brain if any person mentioned liquids I was in fluid land. I went to the Spa, saw all that water. I had to find a public toilet quick. A few days later, I went to the tap dancing class. I missed a couple of steps.

"Hey Eleanor," the instructor said. "You're all wet."

I broke up the chorus line, hurrying to the John. I couldn't even drive on the freeway. I was driving ready to merge onto the freeway and saw this sign Slippery When Wet. I made a fast exist seeking any public facility with a connected bathroom. Listen, I had to quit. Somebody asked me how did I lose all that weight!

"Drinking water eight times a day and eating one meal mid-day!" Yeah, I'm thinner, but let me tell you a little secret. I was constantly searching for a bathroom. I almost lost my job and my man. He told me he did not like his wife too thin. Guess what I found out?" We have a choice of being fat and feeling good, or being thin and looking good."

PLACES WE HAVE LIVED

We have lived in a lot of places. But the most exciting place was San Francisco. We came to California in 1955. In the tradition of the City, all the houses were stacked up on hills. This set of hills was no exception. In fact we called it 'The Hill.' Some people called it 'The Point.' That was no ordinary place. No Sir! They were very selective about who they let live there. They didn't allow any rich folks in there. They didn't allow any middle income people in there. And very few husbands lived there. But it was overloaded with mothers and their children. A bigger problem was the odor that hung in the air. Right on the corner, was the packinghouse, where pigs were slaughtered.

We were packed in our house, too, trying to avoid the stench outside.

Can imagine the next house we moved into? This one had one bathroom with three doors. The third door led to the upstairs dwelling, where the mice lived. We didn't know the house belonged to the mice until we went to bed. Once it was dark, out they scattered from their scared corners wondering who had taken over their space. We torn that house down fast and built a Duplex in its place.

PEOPLE KEPT ASKING ME QUESTIONS

The Civil Rights movement during the 1960's ushered in many requests for African-American speakers who happen to be in any phase of leadership. For the past 15 years I've been going all over California giving lectures on various subjects and especially the race question! I've collected six questions that have been discussed over and over in a multitude of locales. Sometimes I'd be floored, almost speechless. Anybody here tonight from Sebastapol? Good I can tell you these true stories.

"Mrs. Curry. Do you know women's favorite subject?" asked the striking 5'7" blonde young woman.

"Sure women love to talk about men." I responded in a nonchalant tone.

"Will you tell me something?" she appeared serious. "Have you been around men very much?"

"All my life. First my brothers, next some cousins and my uncles. I met a bunch of guys in high school." I'm waiting for her next words.

"Well could you tell me where to find them today?"

"Where have you been looking?"

"I went to the library. I've been doing some research, and I wrote this paper all about men." She sounded desperate now. "So far I haven't really found any men in real life."

"Honey, put that paper away. You are not going to find any men in any library." I was in disbelief. "If you're serious, you need to get rid of that paper. You need to go to places where real men go. Try sporting events, art exhibits and even your local churches."

When we spoke at a Religious Retreat with approximately 500 people in attendance, in Sebastapol, the 'Apple County', I could not believe the next conversation. Remember now, this happen in the early 1960's when we were being called Negroes.

"Mrs. Curry, I've been impressed by the majority of the panels' comments this morning." This matronly stylist woman in a navy blue suit and white blouse with pearls around her neck stated very confident. "I have one problem I'd like for you to address. I don't want my daughter to marry one of them."

"One of them what?" I asked in the best of spirits, keenly listening. There was an embarrassed silence hovering among the participants.
"Ah! You know!" She raised her chin a wee bit higher glaring at me. The audience in the Auditorium was so quiet you could hear a mosquito buzz around the room.

"I'm sorry, but I really don't know," I replied

"Well it starts with an 'N'." She started turning red like a blush or flush.

"I hate to say this. You'll have to give me more information." I'm patiently waiting.

"Negro" she shouted out, exasperated and full of fear. "Could you expound on that?"

"Oh! One of them!" I'm suddenly speechless for a split second. "Let me see now." (The entire group is breathless.) "I've been married to one of them all my adult life and nothing has happen to me yet. Of course I'm not sure what shape he is in."

The entire group burst forth in loud laughter. She snatched her Bible off the seat, yanked her purse close to her body and stormed from the Auditorium. The moderator gaveled for order, announced the need for an ending verse of prayer and the session was over.

One white woman rushed up to me, grabbed me and was hugging me with glee.

"You just saved our women's ministry team from being spilt down the middle."

"What are you telling me?" I asked with concern.

"The woman who asked you the last question had taken a stand that we should not allow any colored people to become members of our church. My daughter is married to a black Marine who came back six months ago. We wanted to have him join our church. This woman started a ruckus expressing her views to keep him out. My daughter refused to go to any place, especially church unless they are together. God bless you for your clear precise answer."

Another speech dealt with raising children.

"I heard you had a house full of kids." This lady appeared very friendly and sincere. "I was told they are lovely children. How did you bring them up to be so pleasant?"

"We did it one day at a time, and by guessing." I smiled briefly. "If things did not work just right, I'd guess I had better do something else. Funny situations happen in life. We used to have eight children at home living in two and three bedrooms. Guess what we have now? We have eight rooms and two kids left. To tell the truth the best way to describe how we raised our kids came from my 26 year old daughter after she moved from our home and was married.

"Mama we sure were lucky to have you and Daddy for our parents. I realize how good Daddy was and is to us." She was animated as she talked. "He taught us so much. He taught us how to be honest, hard-working, loyal, courteous and how to get along with other people."

"Hey, wait just a minute!" I exclaimed slightly alarmed. "What did I teach you?"

"Oh." she laughed continuing. "You taught us how to stay sane while we were learning all that stuff."

Once again I had a request to speak as a panelist about the 'Life of Dr. Martin Luther King. He had been struck by an assassin's bullet in 1968. We were very disturbed due to this unfortunate incident. Of course we wanted to do whatever was necessary to support the needs of his family. The subject was to share how we felt about Dr. King's Dream for America. I felt this would be a great honor. However, I did not know five other people were on the same panel all prepared to speak before me. Can you imagine this scene?

1st Speaker: "I had a dream. I dreamed there were several people running for local government. A couple of them won and are on the City Council. I dreamed they were on Boards and commissions all over the country."

2nd Speaker: "I dreamed they were making more money than ever before. They were buying homes, sending their sons and daughters to college and working at local banking institutions.

3rd Speaker: "I dreamed they were no longer merely the patients in hospitals, they were also the Doctors. They were doing transplants and open heart surgery. They were making new discoveries to prolong life."

4th Speaker: "I don't know how to dream. After Dr. King was killed I lost all hope of freedom becoming a reality. So much is going on, I have not had time to dream. Since I'm here though it would be encouraging if we could learn how to get along with other people."

5th Speaker: "Just between you and me, I'm tired of dreaming. I want some action. Just a little piece of action anywhere! We need to muster up our energy. We need to let Dr. King's family we are still with them."

Now it is my turn. It seems as though everything has been covered. I knew I had to say something powerful. It dawned on me all the panelists were of African descent.

"This evening, my fellow panelists have discussed every conceivable dream one could dare hope to complete in many a lifetime. I am a strong believer in equality. It would please me quite a bit if we have a panel next year to discuss what our white brothers and sisters think about Dr. King's dream. We must seek a balance in our country. We have been separated far too long."

Let the planning begin. The people planned for an entire year. They planned a Luncheon Meeting with two presentations; a Keynote Speaker and ten dancers from the local High School. The Speaker had to be wise, aggressive, strong and an incredible personality. The dancers five on each side remained in the backstage, ready to spontaneously enter the minute the applause ended.

The stage was set. Guess what happen? The man blew the first line. He walked to the lectern. He wiped his brow with a white handkerchief. He mumbled, stumbled through a few casual comments and shouted," I had this nightmare!"

People in the audience started booing and shouting. The man panicked running from the stage. The curtain was quickly closed. Music swiftly filled the air. The curtains were opened fast and the dancers were in place. They began to dance and sing the following song with the beat of the drums.

Dream, dream dream, look up high, you'll love your brother if you try.

Dream, dream dream, do good, you'll see another, no time to cry. Dream, dream, dream, seek peace, pursue it, no need to tell you why. Dream, dream, dream, find hope, spread agape love, until we say good-bye.

The End

ABOUT THE AUTHOR

Eleanor Curry is a Community Activist, Philanthropic Cultivator. Born in St. Louis, Missouri, she was educated at various colleges through independent studies. She attended Antioch College/West, receiving her B.A. Degree in Human Relations. She established the Curry Scholarship Fund for low income teen girls on the Peninsula. Curry lives with her husband in San Carlos, California.

Other books by the author include *"Letters to my Granddaughter"* and *The Courageous Person's Guide to Friendship ABC's of Friendship.*

978-0-595-46804-1
0-595-46804-7

www.ingramcontent.com/pod-product-compliance
Lightning Source LLC
Chambersburg PA
CBHW051216050326
40689CB00008B/1332